Float

Float

Poems by

Ruth Holzer

© 2025 Ruth Holzer. All rights reserved.
This material may not be reproduced in any form, published,
reprinted, recorded, performed, broadcast,
rewritten, or redistributed without
the explicit permission of Ruth Holzer.
All such actions are strictly prohibited by law.

Cover design by Shay Culligan
Cover image by eberhardgoss on Pexels

ISBN: 978-1-63980-734-5

Kelsay Books
502 South 1040 East, A-119
American Fork, Utah 84003
Kelsaybooks.com

Acknowledgments

Grateful acknowledgment is made to the editors of the following publications in which these poems first appeared:

Alabama Literary Review: "New Year's Eve"
Bryant Literary Review: "Ennis"
California Quarterly: "Shrovetide," "The Stranger," "Underground"
The Chaffin Journal: "A Social Life"
Earth's Daughters: "Arundel Gardens"
Exit 13: "Raglan Castle," "Belgooly," "Kinsale," "Old Sweater," "Stripped," "North Pole Road," "A Night at the Blue Lamp"
Freshwater: "The Wandering Shaughnessy"
Glimpse: "The Probable Cause"
Kind of a Hurricane: "January"
Light: A Journal of Photography & Poetry: "A Death in Winter"
Literary Accents: "Days Drawing In"
The London Reader: "Settling In"
The Meadow: "Upper and Lower"
New Croton Review: "Whitsuntide," "Pillar to Post"
Plainsongs: "Float"
POEM: "Near Nogra Junction," "Maybe"
Sojourn: "Freeborn"
Sparks of Calliope: "In Swansea"
Talking River Review: "Curtain Call at the Old Vic"
Third Wednesday: "Stravaging," "All Out"
Trajectory: "In the West," "Mills of the Gods"
U.S. 1 Worksheets: "Wales Forever"
Wilderness House: "At the V&A"

Contents

Lucky Number	13
Freeborn	14
Raglan Castle	15
In Swansea	16
Wales Forever	17
Belgooly	18
Kinsale	19
The Stranger	20
Stravaging	21
Ennis	22
Near Nogra Junction	23
In the West	24
Old Sweater	25
A Night at the Blue Lamp	26
Settling In	27
Float	28
The Man of Bath	29
Upper and Lower	30
One Friday Night	31
Whitsuntide	32
All Out	33
At the V&A	34
Pimpernel Smith at the Cinema in Tooting Bec	35
The Wandering Shaughnessy	36
A Death in Winter	37
Curtain Call at the Old Vic	38
Arundel Gardens	39
Man in a Camel Hair Coat	40
Days Drawing In	41
New Year's Eve	42
A Social Life	43
Underground	44

Matchless	46
January	47
The Probable Cause	48
Maybe	49
Shrovetide	50
Pillar to Post	51
North Pole Road	52
Mills of the Gods	53
Stripped	54

Lucky Number

Eighteen years treading
lightly upon the earth,
still liking it.

Eighteen shillings
for the long-desired book
that would never leave my side.

Eighteen nights and days
I kept myself to myself, until
death came for the maiden.

Freeborn

> *. . . thou art still*
> *The Son of Man in weary Night's decline,*
> *The lost Traveller's Dream under the Hill.*
>   —William Blake, "Of the Gates"

I want it back, the life that late I led,
with my army blanket rolled up tight,
my crazed cup and single change of clothes.
I want to sleep under hawthorn hedges,
in fields of wheat, in fine or wet,
to dream of the distant Beacons,
to walk toward a town called Trapp.

Only wind and clouds in my head,
I shared the farmers' bread and cider,
swearing the system would never get me,
wild as I was for those hills.

I met a young cyclist and freedom
filled my boast. I was beating the system.
I'd never let them grind me down,
the bastards. How I worried and wearied him
all through the night till morning
forced a farewell handclasp. He pressed
a folded ten-pound note into my palm
and raced away. A junior civil servant on holiday,
he must have pitied me, for all the road ahead.

Raglan Castle

The keeper leads me up and around
the moated sandstone ruin,
pointing out the Tudor battlements,
the grass-filled Fountain Court
and the Long Gallery, open to the sky.

He says he's slowly going mad
here in the castle.
His wife died right after he started this job.
He's bored by the few visitors and nothing
to look at but the same old hills of Monmouthshire.

That's his daughter dancing in the shade
of the cracked hexagonal tower
with Rosemary, her black-faced lamb.
When night comes, he assures me,
the adders fall asleep and we'll be safe.

In Swansea

Slag heaps on the outskirts,
cranes busy on the docks,
and in front of The Lord Nelson,
a man with crutches
and a grubby cast on his leg
suggests I come with him
and have a drink. *Why not
enjoy your life,* he says.

Several others loitering there,
emboldened, call out ruder invitations,
though I'm just a traveling person
of fairly decent appearance,
minding my own business on the high street
while buildings rise from the bomb sites.

Wales Forever

With a couple of American tourists I got a ride
out of Swansea, where I had searched for
the lost ghost of a poet, and then I hiked
part of the way down the peninsula
and rode the rest of the way with a gang of carpenters
to the seaside hostel where I stayed for a while
among the cliffs and coves, and built
night fires on the beach with some Australians.

And then I rode back up the peninsula with a fisherman,
then west with a man taking a sick sheep
to be destroyed, and then with a farm inspector
making his rounds, and then with a preacher
who gave me a lecture, and then in a bakery van,
and then with a farmer who put me in the back
of his truck with the sacks of potatoes, and on I went,
deeper and deeper into the purple mountains.

Belgooly

In The Huntsman, I was buying
another round for the sales rep
who'd given me a lift from Cork
in his baby blue Hillman Minx.

After a while, he confided that
he got so flaming lonely on the road.
No company by day or night.
Did I take his meaning?

Soon I was standing again
in a likely spot on the highway
and bidding farewell to him,
the desperate dealer in sheepskin vests

and fleecy slippers, and to Belgooly too,
wide mouth of the ridge, its fields many
diverse shades of green in the shifting light,
its river meandering south to the sea.

Kinsale

Amazing that I made it back to Cork
so quickly. I might have stayed dazed
like a fool at the fair by the side of the road
had not a ginger-haired van driver

from MacMurphy's Monuments
come to deliver me right to the Grand Parade.
He didn't cast odd looks my way
or complain of loneliness, but heartily sang

as we bounced along with the marble angels:
Isn't It Grand, Boys, To Be Bloody Well Dead.

The Stranger

One fine day instead of tramping the roads
with a pack on my back
and my cap pulled down
against the sun and the rain,
I took a rattling green bus
to travel in comfort
through the summer countryside.

My head knocked gently
against the dust-streaked window.
I was the only stranger there
and people began to murmur.
They made sure to sit
well away from me
as though I were contagious.

They whispered their suspicions.
I might be carrying a gun
in my pocket, or a time
bomb. In any case, it was clear
I was up to no good
on the rocky road to Limerick,
that great walled city.

Stravaging

The estuary lay still and gray
beneath a darkening sky.

Around the holy lake
the reeds were hushed.

The great archways of trees
held most of the rain

from me as I kept going
all day, a soft rain

on the stones and the crosses of Rath.

Ennis

The dusty road to Ennis
rose up to meet me
like a blessing,
and when I arrived,
what was there to see
in Ennis, but the inside
of a bus station lavatory
where I rested
until the worst of the day
had passed and then,
still tight as a newt, made for Galway.

Near Nogra Junction

A few sheep grazed on scrubby grass
around a crumbling tower.
Puddles mirrored the low gray clouds.

Old men went by on bicycles
and called out, *Fine day!*
as they rode along the narrow lane
between ditches and drystone walls, and it was.

In the West

I met a man
who knew a man
who knew Yeats:

a dirty geezer toward the end,
shuffling into the Gresham, unshaven,
his trousers held up with a bit of string.

In the West, lingering sunsets
spread over the sea—
peach, plum and granite.

Old Sweater

This sweater owes me nothing,
having already endured a lifetime.
I suspect it will outlast me
and I'll finally pitch over
wrapped inside its thick white wool.

Every stitch has held through circumstance,
stained with malt and ash, the cable pattern
twisting front and back, the cuffs snug,
plenty of room at the waist to grow,
though I had finished growing my twenty years' worth
when I circled the shop in Cork City,
weighing the loss of a few precious pounds
against the certain chill of the night boat passage.

In the end, I decided it bore my name
and pulled it neatly over my head,
inhaling the greasy lanolin,
the rank perfume of leaving.

I wore it into the murk of the lowest deck,
was up at dawn to see the lights of Liverpool.
Welcome to England was what nobody said.
All around me they were shivering and throwing up
    into newspapers.
I leaned forward on the rail, warm and comforted,
watching the stars fade,
listening for the music of what would happen next.

A Night at the Blue Lamp

Past midnight, the last lorry driver
dropped me off in the rain
in the middle of Hemel Hempstead,
a weird crossroad, neither here nor there.
The capital unreachable now
and no other shelter in sight,
I had to try my luck at the door
lit by a constant blue lamp.

This isn't a flippin' hotel,
the duty sergeant advised,
but he let me sleep in a cell in the empty jail.
He threw in a thin brown blanket too,
didn't turn the key, and yet, dead glad
I was to greet dawn through the bars
as the dayshift coppers straggled in.
They hadn't a clue about anything.
They thought they put paid to my roving ways
when they laid my bus fare down.

Settling In

Through an April snowstorm
the taxi made its way, bringing
me with my blue suitcase

to new digs in Ladbroke Grove
and a landlady who laid down
the laws of the house

before showing me the room.
It was another damp box
where I'd eat and sleep alone:

beige wallpaper, grotty carpeting
and a window that didn't close properly
and never would.

I hung my clothes on a cord by the fire,
lived on tea and Jacob's water biscuits,
sinking into what had been decreed.

Float

Along the pre-dawn streets
the milk float glides
in electric near-silence.
The gentle clink of bottles,
the whir of muted wheels
deliver to us as we surface
in the loosening grip
of nightmare or delight,
the recurrent promise
of a day just like the others.

The Man of Bath

I met a cheerful, red-headed
divorcé who declared himself
an actor, singer, playwright and poet.
Of course, we hit it off right away.
Most nights he'd arrive at my door
and we'd make the rounds
of Hampstead and Camden Town,
drinking and gassing about art.
Then he abruptly stopped calling.
I didn't mind that much. Only
he had promised to get me a job
I didn't need papers for
at the dry cleaning plant
where he worked, out Wembley way.

Upper and Lower

Portobello Road, unlovely
main artery of the marginal,
where a woman in a mangy fur jacket
sat by the window of the corner café,
devouring a basin of beets and potatoes,
ceaselessly, breathlessly
pushing in her loaded spoon.
Where a laborer slung his shovelful
of heavy wet cement at the curb
and declared, *The Queen's arse,*
plainly, to no one in particular.

One Friday Night

I probably wouldn't have choked
to death after all, but I could feel
the codfish bone lodged sharply
in the back of my throat,
and neither up nor down would it go,
though I coughed and gulped
in mounting panic. I ran upstairs
and gasped for Mrs. S. to pound my back,
which she handily did, until,
like King Richard the Third
returning to a fateful battle,
I was myself again.

Whitsuntide

Fine weather for the fair on Hampstead Heath,
the Maypole dance,
the jolly tubas and trombones.
There were old folks and babies in prams.

I strayed a little distance off
to rest beneath an ancient oak.
The music mellowed to a thrum,
and I thought of nothing in particular,

only how this day was perfect, even when
a gaunt man on a bicycle stopped by
to rant of Sodom and Gomorrah
and ask could I spare him the price of a pint.

All Out

Sunday on the Serpentine
I glide in a slender scull
beneath the stone bridge
and the trailing willows.

Then I doze on the grass with *The Times*.
Mild light and pigeons fill the afternoon.
I can still afford an ice cream
at the yellow Wall's stand,

perhaps a sugar wafer, too.
I lap it up with a flat wooden spoon
as I meander toward the borders
of royal red marigolds

and the endless plashing
of the fountain, while I pause
by the railings and wonder
what to do with myself.

At the V&A

The torn lining of my raincoat drags
as I hurry in a winter drizzle
through Kensington to take another look
at the Beardsley drawings
before the show moves on:
the lewdness of Lysistrata on full display;
Princess Salomé swirling her peacock skirt,
then, as often happens,
disappointed in the prize,
kissing the lips that did not kiss back.

Pimpernel Smith at the Cinema in Tooting Bec

A scarecrow wearing a greatcoat
and pinstriped trousers is standing
in a field near the labor camp,
and the black-gloved German guard
takes aim with his rifle,
fires a shot to keep the prisoners in order
and for the fun of it,
too far away to notice
the motionless figure's wrist
is dripping blood upon the dusty ground,
for it is really he,
the damned elusive
Scarlet Pimpernel redivivus,
who is really Leslie Howard.

The Wandering Shaughnessy

Slowly and heavily, Mr. S.
treads the stairs from attic
to basement, where he pauses
behind my frosted glass door
with its flimsy lock to check
how late I'm burning their light bulb.
Then all the way up again he paces,
wearing out what night remains.
I hear him on the move till dawn.
He too is plagued by panic,
and often wakes up thrashing in their bed,
screaming, *Lena, Lena,* she told me,
for the mortal fear that is upon him.
And she unable, though she tries,
to soothe with word or touch.

A Death in Winter

Upstairs in the landlord's flat,
I was answering their phone
and keeping the fire going
while Mr. and Mrs. S. stood vigil
at her younger sister's hospice bed.

Later they returned with their story:
a priest had performed the last rites
just as Bridie was fading away.
Nothing could keep her here,
though they held her hands until the end.

I made more tea.
We spoke of heaven and illness,
of her husband and two children
left behind. Worst of all, poor girl,
she'd never see Ireland again.

Curtain Call at the Old Vic

A storm of applause surged
like a mob bent on mayhem.
Cheering, clapping, whistling
and stamping—the crescendo rising,
rising until he came back for a solo call:
white Sir Laurence painted black.

A single beam of light
encircled his powerful body,
still dripping from having murdered
the fair and innocent Desdemona
and from running himself through
with tempered steel.

He nodded to the faceless noise,
bowed low to his worshippers,
his arm a gracious curve,
his Moorish robe
sweeping the stage, so humble,
so arrogant.

Arundel Gardens

I sleep all day, and prowl around at dusk
when crowds desert the Portobello Road
and Notting Hill assumes its wonted gloom.
Between the red-brick library
and the clinic's Gothic spires,
lies a patch of tended greenery,
designed to please the late Victorian eye.

A gardener rakes the fallen leaves
into lofty pyres, sets them ablaze
and banks the fires carefully,
granting gifts of warmth and light
to those of us abroad by night.

Man in a Camel Hair Coat

The belt pulled tight
to display his slenderness
and a black silk foulard
highlighting his pallor,
the genius loci of Notting Hill
and his poodle
made a daily appearance.

Aging, he still dared
to risk his freedom for a jolt of love.
Late at night he'd loiter
near a streetlight by the Underground
anxiously glancing about
until he met another outlaw
or failed to, and retreated into the shadows.

He'd create disturbances in the shops,
ranting that he had better things to do
than stand in line with bloody idiots.
Come, Demon, he'd snap, and leave in a huff.

And often he'd complain that, after
such a tedious wait, he didn't get
the same number of chips as everybody else.

He'd stay there looking aggrieved,
count them aloud and demand two more,
unmoved by the insults
of the lengthening queue.
Head high, he'd saunter off
back to work at the beauty salon,
a celebration of one.

Days Drawing In

Sometimes I missed my former companion,
the boisterous tippler and brawler,
the man of Bath, who dumped
me without warning, leaving me
alone in a small room
to ponder my shortcomings
as another winter came on.

Obviously, I no longer knew
how to behave in a normal situation,
being used to brick walls, abandoned barns,
to drafty stairwells and stubble fields.

I was certain that eventually
I'd relearn the niceties.
In the meantime,
just for the sociability that might be in it,
for the chance of company,
I tried to join Mensa,
but they wouldn't have me either.

New Year's Eve

As the year went slipping down the drain,
Notting Hill became one vast
impromptu masqueraders' ball.
Homeward up the Grove, I struggled past
queens and belted earls, my neighbors all
bedecked in gallantry, or heavy chains

and studded leather. They swirled their cloaks
and flouncy gowns, Rastas, noblemen
or ladies—who could tell or care—
and I among them, fleeing when
a random push turned to a shove and bare
fists roughly handled slower folk.

Back by my hearth, I was unscathed at least,
the single luckless lodger staying here
at No. 80 for the holidays,
reflecting on another wasted year.
The last train rattled empty on its way.
At twelve, a plaintive whistle from the street.

A Social Life

I wasn't alone all the time.
I knew various people
here and there, Australians,
New Zealanders, South Africans,
transients like myself,
who would invite me
now and then to Earl's Court
or Islington for drinks,
inconsequential conversation
and whatever else might occur
entirely without aftermath
in their chill high-ceilinged rooms,
and when I'd had more
than enough of everything,
it was shank's mare
back to the Grove, finding
my way in the kindly dark.

Underground

The escalator slants and rattles down.
You have to focus hard on where you're going
or you'll be felled by green-gilled vertigo.
Clinic signs inquire: *Are You Pregnant?*
as the stairs slope toward their level end:
the lowest depths of Piccadilly Station.

Dug so deeply, Piccadilly Station
could shelter hundreds when the bombs dropped down
and people thought the war would never end—
sirens and ambulances infernally going.
Who knows how many then got pregnant,
embraced in blackout fear and vertigo.

Troubled by a twinge of vertigo,
you board the first train entering the station.
Now you really wonder if you're pregnant,
your good luck failing, or your guard let down.
You lose track of where this train is going
and what you mean to do there at the end.

You know it won't be long before the end.
Clattering backward, whirled in vertigo,
you dream of better places to be going.
Gangs of men burst in at every station,
appraisingly, they look you up and down,
their glances hinting that you're pregnant.

Your daily prayer is never to get pregnant,
to stay unreplicated till the end;
inviolate, although you did stoop down,
surrendering once to vulgar vertigo.
Your room was too close to the station;
people were always coming and going

and then they were mostly going,
leaving you alone and maybe pregnant.
You can get anywhere from any station,
Clapham Common unto far Hatch End.
Thinking of these networks gives you vertigo.
No one will notice if you fall down,

so you keep going, reckless to the end.
Happily not pregnant, resisting vertigo,
you find another station and ride down.

Matchless

My Aunt Fanny had a friend who knew
an executive at the lighter company
that had its European headquarters
here in smoky London, and she persuaded him
to put in a good word for me
with Human Resources.

Dressed for success, on the appointed day
I sallied forth to the Strand and found
the historic, high-windowed building.
They let me stew an hour in an anteroom
embellished with fake heraldry,
before informing me that they had,

to their sincere regret, no suitable opening,
neither in these plush offices
nor at their factory in Leatherhead.
I got instead a bird's-eye view of my twilit city,
the river milky with mist. Not having the fare,
I walked all the way home. I would never give up.

January

Along the Embankment,
merging with the evening fog,
a pallid regiment of vagrants
stared out from their cardboard shelters.
Had I anything to give,
I would have, and gladly,
in honor of the kindness of strangers,
and to spare at least one of them
from scavenging the frozen trash
for tonight's sustenance.
But I was following too closely,
my hands hollow and raw.

The Probable Cause

In that record winter,
an infection struck my eyes.
They oozed mucus, puffed
almost shut, ached and burned,
one at a time or both at it together.
Through the white mist of morning
I blundered, and the dense fog
of evening; at night I lay
with a warm rag pressed over my face.
Later I'd peer at pulsing lines of print,
Ruskin or Thackeray, until at last,
sleep would seize me. Once
Mrs. S. poked her head round the door
and declared it must have come
from reading too much.

Maybe

On this rainy afternoon,
another letter from my father
arrives, accusing me
of squandering my irreplaceable time
by staying here so long,
purposeless. Maybe he's right.
And maybe I'll just add it to the collection
and think about something else.
On the other side of the wall
a Jamaican woman is singing—
a bright lost bird among the dripping trees.

Shrovetide

In my cabbage-colored room
through short February days
and nights with no tomorrow,
I worked at something or nothing,
nourished by doubt.

Early one Tuesday, Mrs. S.
brought down a plate of pancakes,
egg-rich, buttery golden,
each curled like a wish, sweetened
with the finest sugar,
all a-swim in lemon juice.
It was America at home.

Pillar to Post

Preparatory to a divine service,
they were lighting candles
in the nave and the side chapels
of the great cathedral,
and ejected the oblivious person
reading funerary inscriptions
who strolled down to Chelsea,
off-season for the Flower Show,
past the Royal Hospital
and the pensioners mumbling on benches,
then paced the length of Tite Street,
its fame recalled by round blue plaques
affixed to many of the houses,
names of the great and the good
long since decamped,
and followed in the tracks
of the sublime Oscar
along the river walk,
the tide going out,
the light slowly failing,
and back by way of St. James's Park
where I scattered my supper crusts
to the ragged sparrows.

North Pole Road

Chimneys thrust into a cindery sky
above a stretch of soot-stained wall,
trash-blown lots, a stumbling row
of condemned houses, shuttered shops,
an overpass sprayed with magenta genitalia.

I thought I'd go take a look at the Scrubs,
since I had seen everything else in the city,
but turned back at the end of this unredeemed way.
My room in the Grove seemed welcoming then;
the drab from the squalid more clearly discerned.

Mills of the Gods

Mrs. S. washed my window
once, and I was able to observe
with greater accuracy
the rain churning
her backyard into mud
as well as the faint light
that followed, striking
the liver-colored brick wall
at sunset and making it glow
for a moment with false warmth.
I watched both of these things
for a not inconsiderable period of time,
and at last it occurred to me
that one might declare
the entire enterprise
crowned with failure.

Stripped

The night before departure,
as I lay my room bare,
what bouts of remorse I endure,
what half-baked vows of betterment.

Untacked from the walls,
my crossed-off calendar
and the vivid picture postcards
of cathedrals and castles.

All that remains is the wooden crucifix
Mrs. S. had nailed above the bed.
It gazes sadly down on me,
having, as it were, the last word.

About the Author

Ruth Holzer is the author of several chapbooks, most recently *Living in Laconia* (Gyroscope Press, 2021) and *Among the Missing* (Kelsay Books, 2021). Her poems have appeared in *Blue Unicorn, Freshwater, Journal of New Jersey Poets, POEM,* and *Slant,* among other journals and anthologies. She has served as a co-editor of *Haibun Today* and as an associate editor of *tinywords.*

A multiple Pushcart Prize and Best of the Net nominee, she's received the Edgar Allan Poe Memorial Prize from the Poetry Society of Virginia, the Tanka Splendor Award, and the Ito En Art of Haiku Contest Grand Prize.

www.ingramcontent.com/pod-product-compliance
Lightning Source LLC
Chambersburg PA
CBHW031206160426
43193CB00008B/521